WHAT REMAINS

Other Books by the Author

POETRY

Midrashim

Dovchik

The View from Jacob's Ladder

ANTHOLOGIES

Modern Poems on the Bible: An Anthology

The Gospels in Our Image: An Anthology of Twentieth Century Poetry

TRANSLATIONS

Eustache Deschamps: Selected Poems
(translated with Jeffrey Fiskin)

Astonishments: Selected Poems of Anna Kamienska
(edited and translated with Grazyna Drabik)

What Remains

Selected Poems

DAVID CURZON

Teaneck, New Jersey

Copyright ©2021 David Curzon. All rights reserved. No
part of this book may be used or reproduced in any manner
whatsoever without written permission except in the case of
brief quotations embodied in critical articles and reviews.

Published by Ben Yehuda Press
122 Ayers Court #1B
Teaneck, NJ 07666

http://www.BenYehudaPress.com

Jewish Poetry Project #13
http://jpoetry.us

To subscribe to our monthly book club and support independent
Jewish publishing, visit https://www.patreon.com/BenYehudaPress

ISBN 978-1-953829-11-5
cover photograph by
Set in Adobe Jenson by Raphaël Freeman MISTD, Renana Typesetting

Contents

A View of Manhattan	1
Uncertainty	2
Instructions to a Seed	3
The Grave	4
Three Old Symbols	6
An Open Fire	7
A Top	8
The Emigrant	9
The Tao of Water	10
Home	11
A Marriage	12
An Old Master	13
The News	14
Confession of Faith	15
The Chosen People	16
An Office at Night	17
Recognizable Essence	18
Prince Approaching Standing Goddess	19
Instructions from the Mustard Seed Manual	20
The Ant	21
Psalm 1	22
Yahrzeit	23
The Gardens	27
Friends in the Art	29
A Flint Arrowhead	30
The Blameless	32

Your Last Letter	34
Bird on a Rock	35
To King David	36
Fossil	37
The Book of Job	38
A Moment	39
Approaching Fifty	40
Forgive Me	41
An Australian Childhood	42
An Assyrian Seal	43
Michèle and Ronsard	45
Sundry Lessons of the Exodus	46
At the Sea of Reeds	47
Pompeii	48
Correspondences	49
In Japan	50
In the British Museum	53
In the Nezu Museum	54
The Importance of Ecology	55
Once Upon a Time	56
Two Calls	58
Mencius, More or Less	59
Five Careers in the Middle Kingdom	60
Advice	62
Predictions That Will Come True	63
Aphorisms in a Sufi Spirit	64
Wu Wei	65
In the Freer Gallery	66
The Afterlife of Ramesses the Great	67
An Ancient Egyptian Lady	68
Classical Moments	69
Last Things	70
An Obituary	71
Yiddish Teleologies	72

Conjoint Gods	73
Babylonian Identities	74
The Root of All Evil	75
Eden, Upstate New York	76
The Life and The Good	77
Before the Throne of Judgment	78
The Theology of the Big Bang	79
If You Do Well	80
Make an Ark	82
The Existential Ant	83
The Need to Dissemble	84
Blessings and Curses	85
The Days of the Years of Your Life	86
Loving Your Neighbor	87
Benedictions	88
Justice	89
Ten Other Commandments	90
Four of Freud's Antiquities	91
Gods of the "A" List	92
A Cold Palm Reading	93
The Insects	94
The Auction of Lot 68	95
Is It Worship?	96
Cardiovascular Facts and Fates	97
Why Bring Us Here to Die?	98
Scholar Rocks	99
Someone Explains Himself	100
It's Been One Year	101
Three Consolations	103
The Life You Had	104
Acknowledgments	105
About the Author	107

A View of Manhattan

As I looked out
a dusk window
there was slight traffic
in channeled patterns
between the fixed
silent vigil
of other buildings
and I became,
by the illusion
of mere reflection,
imposed upon them.

But evening darkened.
Their lights appeared.
They slowly formed
galaxies of yellows
that stared at me,
confronting presumption
with inviolate silence,
like the worshipped stars
above Babylon
in the beginnings
that led to this.

Uncertainty

Heisenberg's a legend
because he pointed out
that all our finest measurements
contain a certain doubt.

A little doubt is certain,
that's the word he used,
Uncertainty his Principle,
and this is what he proved:

what we measure's made of
what we measure with,
atoms disturb atoms
and precision is a myth.

So take some care, my darling,
don't look too close at me,
the impulse of your measure
provokes uncertainty.

Instructions to a Seed
(*Matthew 13:7*)

Don't worry; you're now
in darkness and very small
but you have it in you.
There's nothing to do except

grow. You've got to draw
your only nourishment
from whatever surrounds you.
You can't change location.

If you *fell among thorns* it's
too bad; you'll be stifled
or die. No one will care:

there are so many seeds
that are also in darkness
with dispositions. Just grow.

The Grave

I
There was the grave, a gravel top, no slab,
and at his head, in Hebrew and English scripts,
"Brother of Tola" – who also killed herself –
"Father of David" – who doesn't quite know now

why he is here, except to photograph
the setting and the stone, and pull a weed
in what seems otherwise a well-kept plot,
and stir the gravel with his fingertips.

The trees have thickened in these twenty years
and even in unyielding cloudless heat
the avenue they form is all in shade

inviting the eye to something it forgot,
the little lodge where the brief service was
now empty. Locked. I rattled at the door.

II
And then I left and flew through Athens.
I had a single afternoon to see again
the statues from the Cyclades, the mask of gold,
the classic marbles, the rock crystal bowl,

and to be shocked by grave-stone fragments
I must have glanced at twenty years ago.
Each stele portrays the person gone and those
remaining, and the farewell gestures they

wished to record in sculpture's deep relief.
Some showed eyes meeting, other eyes looked down,

and in one stele the dead man stretched his hand
toward the living, whom he almost reached.

How civilized to visit if the grave
contained this reaching outward, back to life.

III
Mosaic law of course forbids such art
which risks idolatry. In any case
there was no reaching out, no note was found
beside your tiny bottle's missing pills.

I davened Kaddish at your open grave,
a mourner's prayer which doesn't mention death
or offer gestures but in praise refers
to the world created as it had been willed.

And so I'm left with memories. One time
you let me in your darkroom to take part
in your enlargements and developing.

I still recall the shudder when I saw,
drowned in solution in that shallow tray,
blank paper slowly come to show a face.

Three Old Symbols

The wound-up thread he held played out until
Theseus found, within his maze, the beast he had to kill.

Shiva, dancing in a ring of flame,
treads down the demon that his dance must tame.

In darkness Jacob wrestled with a stranger who
did not prevail, and blessed him, when their night was
    through.

An Open Fire

The source that now warms me
had kindling as tinder
and divulges disquiet
by a sap's incantation,
a distracted flaming,
and I, like all others,

am wooed by these wavers
of shapely persistence,
an urging upward
as obvious and hidden
as every vocation's
gradient of blazing.

A Top

Here is an object fit for meditation:
an energetic balanced operation
maintaining its own useless, doomed, unstable
and charming act as long as it is able.

The Emigrant

Like millions before me who weren't explorers
I fled my birthplace, a person urged on
    by what I fled from:

pogroms, or the prospect of conscription into
a life in regimen to relentless authority,
    a czarist army,

and – yes – from frock coats, an ankle-length blackness,
the unclean closeness of home and custom,
    the mud of the shtetl,

but also from song, generations along
ceremonial tables, a familiar family
    of ready blessings

for simple actions – lighting candles,
dividing bread – my great forsaking
    for the sake of alien freedom.

The Tao of Water

The creek's clear water,
apt at passivity,
virtually invisible,
prefers to circumvent
if possible but is
inquisitive, enters
crevices, little
splits, flows
over stones
endlessly caressing
as it continues
to wear away
all opposition.

Home
(*Australia*)

The center of the land in which I came to life
is unremitting red desert stretching
its monotonous prospect to thin horizons,
an aridity as immense as most other countries

but when rains come they come in torrents
creating rivers which pour into vast depressions,
lapsed lakes that wait for replenishment
which returns to them their name and purpose

and then the desert displays what was dormant within it,
the grass seed preserved throughout parched seasons,
and yields a springtime that even has flowers
until heat evaporates the reaches of water

and once more rivers and lakes dry out to depression
and loam desiccates to hard clay
and winds traverse that unperturbed surface,
the heart of the land in which I came to life.

A Marriage

There must have been some moments. What remains?

The honeymoon: I woke in that spacious room
while she was sleeping, eased out of the bed
and opened up one blind and in the dawn
I watched the renewals of her breathing form.

Returning, I'd cleared customs: there she was
the only person in the crowd beyond
the barrier, then she caught sight of me
and all her waiting body waved her wave.

The separation: we'd been out at night,
had come back home in silence, just got in,
when she, while taking off her coat, had turned
and told me simply, "I've decided." Yes,

that moment, too, is part of what remains.

An Old Master

Who needs vast canvasses with battle scenes
or even small ones with a hundred souls
in hell or heaven or waiting in between?
A head and shoulder portrait is enough,
it shows me everything I want to see,
the face up close, a stubble-chinned old man
whose wrinkled grin insists on some response.

That's what I thought when I was twenty-one.
Now in museums I often find myself
lingering in front of scenes of innocents
being speared. I'm also curious
about those crowds in hell – they're so diverse!
And yet I still come back to that old man
and still, of course, don't know quite what to say.

The News

When I switched on the TV news last night
it showed a woman in El Salvador
draped in black shapeless peasant clothes
mourning her eldest son's assassination
by beating her head against his gravestone,
her body shaking with sobs' convulsions,
and from a distance of two thousand miles
I watched the action of her rib-cage spasms,

that motion imposed on her by our nature,
and felt sobs about to rise even in me
and did not breathe to stop my body's autonomy
as I had when I heard the news of my father's death
but allowed myself to weep at another's grief
and learned my condition from an unknown mother.

Confession of Faith
(*for Stanley Barkan*)

Yes, I believe
we are no longer
residing in paradise.

Yes, I believe
it would have been better
to have never eaten
knowledge of evil.

Yes, I believe
history contains
a deluge drowning
almost all.

Yes, the decision
not to permit
our kind to acquire
eternal life
has, I believe,
gained vindication.

The Chosen People

The Hebrews in Egypt who chose not to leave –
mostly those holding appointed positions –
refused to be part of a stampeded populace
led by a mad stuttering murderer
who discoursed in the desert with burning bushes.
These realistic skeptics expected the worst;
they could predict worship of golden calves.
It made sense to them to stay civilized slaves

and not be witness to the separating sea,
the pillar of cloud as guide by day,
the pillar of fire as guide by night,
the struck rock that gushed water,
the thunder and lightning as signs over Sinai
the glow of Moses descending the mountain.

An Office at Night
(*circa 1980*)

It's late; the day's waste has been taken;
the solitary cleaner has vacuumed all corridors.
The leather reception couches, the long conference table,
the boardroom's world maps, are now merely a furniture of
unlit areas. And the enclave of confidential documents
is locked, the way barred by metal gates.
I have a key to its secrets but don't need them.
My desk is littered with memoranda, transcripts of
    meetings.
I draft with selected instruments: dark leads,
masking tapes, erasers that leave no trace.
Half my effort is over, the outline is clear.
I pause, re-examine discarded passages, pick up
sharp barber's scissors, shear between
disparate thoughts, and collate them in other contexts.

And now I glance at the wall opposite, at
the African masks I have chosen to confront me:
a monkey's visage reduced to one huge grin;
a disk consisting of eyes, mouth and horns –
vision, ingestion and defense, rudimentary essentials.
And on a small table is a Baule statue,
a man standing with thick legs spread apart,
arms bent, hands clasped in front
grasping both sides of an extended beard,
a reflexive position, self-contained, stable,
an ancestor figure with austere features, abstracted
as any animal, his pose dominating the silence
of this late night with simple presence, with
character issuing from stance alone.

Recognizable Essence
(*for Jeffrey Fiskin*)

How rapidly a culture seems to reach
recognizable essence! Even a creature
in grey earthenware from an early dynasty
with a row of horns and a curled tail, a thing
not living in the Land of the Three Dragons,
stands stable on four legs
looking down at the ground nearby
unconcerned with the world outside its circle
in a stance expressing secular dignity.
And later came Kuan-yin and his
position of royal ease – right wrist
resting on a raised knee, hand pointing
downward, fingers spread out, separated,
unstrained, a body balanced by
the stretch of left arm to grounded palm –
an alert aristocrat, a symbol needing
no esoteric explanation. And then the millennium
of ink painting, the great inspirations:
Travelers Among Mountains, Waterfall in Autumn,
Sparrow Resting on Apple Branch,
Village in Clearing Mist, Bamboo in the Wind
"standing on the solitary mountain, dignified,
quiet, typifying a will of nobility,
painted and written with a light heart by
        Wu Chen."

Prince Approaching Standing Goddess

In this Egyptian low relief
of ochre stone with quartz inclusions
a prince approaches a standing goddess
named in the inscription simply as
"Lady of Heaven, Mistress of the Gods."

Her profile shows us an erect full breast
and a belly button dimpled just above
the sheath skirt making obvious
the contours of her soft but compact bottom.
She smiles at him, entirely confident.

The young prince doesn't smile;
his lips are straight, his gait is stiff;
he's focusing – God help him – on Approach;
been dead for more than twenty centuries.
The quartzite sparkles, winking as I pass.

Instructions from the Mustard Seed Manual
(on Chinese landscape painting)

Each scene should include unattainable regions
and places where the sage would wish to linger.
Paths should have evident beginnings and ends
with extended stretches hidden by turnings.
Mist and clarity must both exist.
Do not show limits to shallow waters.

Among mountains some peaks are low;
don't treat peach trees as though plum.
For trees with many, add branches;
for those with few, reduce further.
And portray old trees with exposed roots,
living in rock, clinging to cliffs.

Landscape should contain habitation.
Outline with style, leave out trifles:
a glimpse of gate gives the wish to enter;
in a mountain residence the inner rooms
need not be seen to show seclusion.
A terrace should not be left empty.

Take as your own some ancient inscription:
Sitting on a rock, watching the stream.
Listening to a lute on the other shore.
With hands behind, walking in autumn.
Alone in the open, reciting a poem.
Scholar crossing bridge on donkey.

The Ant
(*Proverbs 6:6*)

Go to the ant, thou sluggard,

and watch it lug an object
forward single file
with no short breaks for
coffee, gossip, a croissant,

and no stopping to apostrophize
blossom, by-passed because
pollen is not its job,
no pause for trampled companions:

consider her ways – and be content.

Psalm 1

Blessed is the man not born
in Lodz in the wrong decade,
who walks not in tree-lined shade
like my father's father in this photo, *nor
stands in the way of sinners* waiting for
his yellow star,
nor sits, if he could sit, in their cattle car,

but his delight is being born
as I was, in Australia, far away,
and on God's law he meditates night and day.

He is like a tree that's granted
the land where is it planted,
that yields its fruit by reason
of sun and rain in season.

The wicked are not so, they
burn their uniforms and go their way.

Therefore the wicked are like Cain
who offered fruit which God chose to disdain.

And the way of the righteous is Abel's, whose
sacrifice God chose to choose
and who was murdered anyway.

Yahrzeit

I
I'd fixed a time
to view the body
and entered that room
empty except for
the central coffin,
its top resting
against the trestle.

A white cloth was
pulled back from your
unearthed face.

Your cheeks shone;
your mouth was open;
your teeth protruded;

like the head I'd gazed at
in a book you gave me
for my bar mitzvah,
Gods, Graves, and Scholars,
which described the findings
of those who uncovered
where we had come from:
the face of a mummy
after its binding
had been undone.

II
I keep alive
you at my bedside
reciting Byron,

and your accent
on each beat,
and your pause
before the rhyme word
to let me follow
"fold" with "gold";
and our delight
in verse concerning
the two brains of
long Brontosaurus,
one in front
and one at the back
to catch thoughts
the head had missed;
and an early evening
while you were cooking
and I brought crayons
to the kitchen table,
and made up creatures
my mind imagined
when you had read me
"What varied being
peoples every star,"
and your soft comment
while tossing salad,
not disapproving,
perhaps surprised at
the fact of difference,
"I'd always thought
Pope meant their god";
and you transcribing
on a cardboard bookmark
the stray stanza
that took my fancy,

which you found at last
in Swinburne's collected
eleven hundred pages.

After thirty years
when I emptied
your bedroom's bookcase
I came on that marker.
I saw the ink
absorbed by cardboard.
Your clear writing
had bled and blotted.

III
The books you'd borrowed
from the local library
were in the kitchen;
when I returned them
the head librarian
fought back her tears
to say: "Your mother was
a scholarly lady."

IV
I now keep a photograph of you
on the table opposite my apartment entrance
and pass it as I enter and as I leave
and at each glance I get a small
stab, the physical effect as it registers.

V
I have a favorite jacket which I'd frayed
around the cuff. The tailor in New York
suggested that I throw the thing away

adding, "This garment isn't dying it
is dead." And so it would have been but I
took it back home to you the visit

which was the last, and watched you straighten out
the broken threads, and line them up, and then
bind your mending with stitches of a fine
matched cotton, so that now I have to search
with some of the same care you gave to it
to see your hand in fabric you had touched.

The Gardens

*By the rivers of Babylon, There we sat down, yea,
we wept, when we remembered Zion. (Psalm 137:1)*

Melbourne's Botanical Gardens, where I came
to walk along the bordered paths with him,
and pose in short pants for the photos placed
into this album I'm now leafing through,
and eat my sandwiches besides the lake,
and cast bread on the waters for the swans.
And later, when we met on Sundays, we
went off to European movies, then
to his small room where we played chess. He cut
his dense black bread held close up to his chest.
One afternoon we passed a synagogue
and saw some litter scattered on its steps
including lobster shells. He said, "This is
deliberate desecration. They must know
lobster isn't kosher." "Daddy, it's not that,
it's an Australian picnic not cleaned up."
I thought it was absurd he didn't understand.

This must have been round nineteen fifty-five.
A mere ten years had passed. And in four years
he'd suicide, and I would read the documents
he kept inside their envelopes in a wood box –
certificates of immigration, change
of name, degrees, but mainly photographs
and letters from his parents and his friends.
And then I found a letter he had sent
to Poland. The final one. It said, "I wish
I could protect you from the sadists" and was stamped
UNABLE TO DELIVER. Somehow I

was not aware. He never talked of it.
And now I try to visualize what happened to
his parents and those smiling friends of his,
and try to understand how it would feel
orphaned, divorced, recalling, to walk in
the gardens of Babylon, and not weep.

Friends in the Art

If only I could feel at home somewhere

and meet friends in a café for a drink
and joke, concoct a project, read to them
my latest composition, help write up
another manifesto on our art.

Didn't this happen once in the salons
of Paris or St. Petersburg, around
the court at Weimar, in the back room of
the Mermaid Tavern with Ben Jonson there,

in the agora at the time of Socrates,
the gardens of Ming literati near Suzhou?
These friends I've read about, they did exist
and meet and talk and joke and write and drink

in places where, surely, they felt at home.

A Flint Arrowhead
(*for Bert Gross*)

This sharp heart
was shaped in the late
stone age
by a skilled sculptor
who scooped minute
serrations in
the thin flint
at the edges of
his arrowhead,
who shaved bevels
on the waist at its base,
who directed his
precious tools
in dozens of other
evident incisions,
including some
finishing touches
not needed
for mere hunting.

Such craftsmen would
after much progress
be replaced by
men of metal,
molders, who
forced ore
out of its hiding
in hard places,
melted it
into submission,
poured it

in standard patterns
at foundries founded
on the labor of burned
and blistered slaves.

My anonymous colleague
who chipped away
at your mundane trade
to produce this
unused shape
which looks as if
it would break on bone
or even in
the attempt to penetrate
a bison's hide,
another someone
has come to comprehend
something of your
crafted heart.

The Blameless
(*Psalm 119*)

Blessed are those whose way is blameless, but
do they exist? The evidence is bleak.
Adam and Eve of course, don't fill the bill;
and the first murderer's no good, although
he got protection; Abel didn't last –
to have a blameless life you have to live –
and Noah, "righteous in his generation," was,
the rabbis tell us, righteous only when
compared with those God wiped out in the Flood;
and Abraham talked back, and tried to kill his son,
and threw a helpless woman and her child
into the desert with one loaf of bread,
and served non-kosher when God came to lunch;
and Sarah laughed at God and beat the servants; Lot
committed incest at least twice while drunk;
and passive Isaac much preferred the son
God didn't want; and Jacob, as we know,
stole, although his inability
to bargain when in love redeems him in my eyes;
and Joseph as a child was an obnoxious brat
and later was a prig and, when he had the chance,
tortured his father over Benjamin;
and Moses was a murderer in his youth,
which could perhaps be justified, but still
he had a temper, smashed the stones on which
God had engraved commandments for us all,
and, after, ordered a general massacre.
Should I go on? Joshua's atrocities
have turned much stronger stomachs than my own.
And David? He's no prig, for sure, and who am I
to hold adultery against him, but

to send the husband to the front and have him killed
was, I must be frank with you, not nice.

I come back to the psalm, which asks (verse nine)
How can a young man keep his way pure?
And the ladies have their problems too, I know.

Your Last Letter

I
Your writing was mature; you had evolved
a script which was your own but not at all
idiosyncratic; your characters
were separate and clear but each linked up
with others in your way. And now the impulses
forming your letters and their links are gone.
Nobody is at your kitchen table now
adding a few lines to an aerogramme,
noting the dates which marked each entry off.
Your letters mixed in quotes from Lucan with
family news, the weather, medical complaints.
Your writing was mature; you had evolved.

II
And now
once more
I've picked up
your last letter.

And now
once more
I've opened up
your last letter.

And now
once more
I've read
"My darling Dov."

And now
no more.

Bird on A Rock
(*for Itzhak Galnoor*)

I envy this squat black bird that is so
unreasonable, confident, is so
without a doubt that it deserves to be,
and would, could, never falsify himself to be
other than what he was, and is: a crow

To King David
(*Psalm 8*)

I know, my namesake, you didn't write
all the psalms, and certainly not those howls
from out of Babylon, the first exile
where remnants of your nation, stunned,
adjusted after the first destruction.
And yet these Praises – the collection's name –
and petitions, arguments, and more straightforward
cries, are rightly (so I feel) ascribed to you
since, it turns out, you were, your reign and Solomon's,
our people's brief glory.
                              Yet I and other poets don't
envy you for that, not even for
the life which wrung composition out of you,
but for the settings in temples, synagogues,
monasteries, cathedrals, hospices,
in which your Praises have been chanted, sung,
recited, read, whispered, remembered, in
the night before a battle, near sick beds,
in prisons, slave plantations, gulags, the death camps;
and for the harps, pipes, cymbals, strings,
named in the short last psalm that someone wrote,
some lucky poet, who might have heard it as
Priests walked up the Temple steps to where
they'd splash the sacrificial blood and still,
three thousand years beyond those Bronze Age rites,
it still is chanted by the descendants who now live
in Melbourne, Buenos Aires, New York, Tel Aviv,
who also sing a simple line of yours which says
How glorious is Your name in all the earth.

Fossil

Should I envy this fossil fish
embedded in stone with only
skeleton left, the backbone
that gave him, while alive,

structure, sufficient rigidity
to permit a swift correction
of path, and ribs that protected
a simple heart and the tracts

of other inward parts,
with what remains being
a readable essence revealed

as it never was in the brief
living, fixed and oblivious
in the rock where it continues?

The Book of Job
(*A summary*)

God, on a whim, indulges the logic
of Satan's speculation that Job's true nature
cannot be known until tested.

It's an experiment: Job's children
are killed, etcetera, etcetera,
and the pious victim pines for death.

Job's wife suggests, "Curse God and die"
which, given what we know
and she didn't, seems an approach
to the problem of evil as sensible as any.

Job's friends are silent for seven days
respecting his grief, and then they
attempt to comprehend. One friend recalls
a night vision, a Voice saying
"Can mortal man be more just than God?" –
an angle of argument not too far from
the answer of the Whirlwind which convinced Job.

Job, who howled and didn't listen
to his friends' honest efforts at understanding
is lavishly rewarded. His friends are punished
for wrong reasoning. Satan, whose hypothesis
was, after all, worth testing, is ignored.

Creatures trying to see reason in His Whims
irritate the Master of Universe.

A Moment
(*Michèle and Proverbs 15:23*)

Winter. Fifth Avenue. Half a block south
of Central Park. It blurted out. Ten years ago.
"You're as lovely as the falling snow."

A man hath joy in the answer of his mouth.

And you were startled by what you understood

and, spoken in their moment, words are good.

Approaching Fifty
(*Deuteronomy 8*)

And you shall remember all the way

one or two early intimations:
turning back (at four, on a family picnic)
to examine a single pink wildflower,
and then running to catch up with the others;
stooping (at seven, a beach in Queensland)
to scrutinize an unusual shell and be
shocked when I noticed it was broken;

these forty years in the wilderness

and then, after her death, sorting through
a drawer in her dressing table, I recognized
a simple scarf I'd given my mother
had touched her
              to humble you, to test you,
to know what was in your heart.

Forgive Me
(*i.m. Lillian Curzon, 1919–1986*)

Forgive me, Lillian, for not following
the impulse of the moment when I found
inside your handbag after you died
that familiar edition of Sir Thomas Browne's
Religio Medici and leafed through it
reading passages marked by
slight pencil lines in the margin
which seemed yours because they were
at the edge of sentiments that would appeal –
would have appealed – to you and so
I took it to the cemetery intending
to give a quick speech and then
say over your open grave
some of the thoughts you'd kept inside
your bag, but I became worried that
Browne's diction would be difficult
and the grave was dug and the mud
oozed around our shoes
and the crowd of mourners was too
spread out and so I gave my speech
in a silence like the silence between us
in your last years and it is
nineteen months since you died and I
found just now in Borges' poems
a sonnet to Browne and of course I thought
of that small blue volume and your
bedside table piled with books
and your handbag and the pencil lines and my
not saying what I had wanted to say.
I miss you in death as I did in life.

An Australian Childhood

When I woke
I was greeted by
the laughter of
the kookaburras

and white cockatoos
and red galahs
flew in their dozens
among the gumtrees

and the fresh leaves
I picked and crushed
perfumed my fingers
with eucalyptus

and up above,
shy and hidden,
nibbling the leaf-tips,
koalas were feeding

and the stinging of
a bull-ant's bite
was eased by the sap
of snapped bracken

and when I woke
I was greeted by
the laughter of
the kookaburras.

An Assyrian Seal
(*for Gail, on turning fifty*)

When I was in Jerusalem last year
I went as usual to old Zadok's shop –
the only dealer in antiquities who is,
all other dealers grudgingly admit,
an honest man – and rummaged round in his
dusty, ill-lit and littered wonderland,
a chaos of cardboard boxes filled
with Roman oil lamps and scarab amulets
and even well-preserved black pots that came
from the Iron Age.
                He sits at the back
behind a desk piled high with metal drawers
containing bits of opalized old glass
and dice from Byzantium and Roman rings
of low-grade silver and patinated bronze
in every size, including mine. He also has
hundreds of Greek and Roman and Jewish coins
all mixed together in bowls which he upturns
above black velvet laid with a flourish on
a patch of countertop that he sweeps clean
so I can search again – I know it is
sentimental – for the crude designs
minted in caves in the Judean hills
of the doomed Jewish revolt against the Romans
to end up always buying two or three
fine heads of the conquerors with (yet again)
beauty, however bloodstained, winning out
over the call of blood.
                Last year I bought this seal
from the "Assyrean pearoid" (as you
can see from the certificate) which was

incised with what appears to be an animal —
you can press it on clay to make it out
or get an expert to make an expert guess —
about three thousand years ago, give or take
a century or two, and who can be exact
when it's millennia we're talking of
or even the fifty years that we have now
persisted as we rummage on among
the residue of conscious life on one
blue planet circling a little sun.

Michèle and Ronsard

We were ambling hand in hand in Central Park
hoping to buy a bag of roasted chestnuts
and taking photos of each other so close up
that all the autumn foliage was out of focus

with you in a little woolen pixie cap
reciting *La solitaire vie, et le désert sejour*
valent mieux que la Cour and laughing as we
wandered off in search of the great Ronsard

and I got agitated because it wasn't possible
to find even one of the sonnets for Hélène
in the Sunday bookstalls on Fifth Avenue

but you hushed me with *"Amour dans les déserts*
comme aux villes s'engendre, and isn't this afternoon
more important to us than all Ronsard's sonnets?"

Sundry Lessons of the Exodus

Something will guide you: if not fire, a cloud.
You're a mixed multitude, don't be too proud.
You'll be pursued by what you leave behind.
This wilderness is where you'll be divined.
The water here is bitter; make it sweet.
Eat the strange food; it's all you have to eat.

At the Sea of Reeds
(*Exodus 14:11–22*)

It is said:

In each generation we exodus from Egypt,
reach the Sea of Reeds, look in back in fear,
and protest to whoever led us there:
Why bring us to this desert just to die!
We'll kill ourselves by drowning in the Sea!
We'll return to slavery and escape annihilation!
We'll shout, frighten them with noise!

But that generation – so goes another Midrash –
stopped their complaint against circumstance
and entered those waters up to their toes,
up to their ankles, up to their knees,
up to their lips, up to their nostrils,
and only then did the miracle occur.

Pompeii

The ancient world was so much like our own.
Its rutted streets were walked and in now empty rooms
people sat down and argued, ate. Or, like the day
I wandered round, were lonely in Pompeii.

Correspondences

Where have I found my correspondences?

In a spare landscape by Ni Tsan which shows
an empty pavilion on a riverbank
shaded by half a dozen slender trees,
"six gentlemen" the Chinese scholars call them,
all sketched with a dry brush, and beyond the other bank
are his low mountains and the vacant sky;

and in wet brushstrokes by the eccentric monk
Bada Shanren, "the old man of the hills,"
who painted crazed black myna birds
and fish with eyes which seem to glare
in angry accusation at those blank
stretches of paper they are floating in;

and in the famous landscape by Fan K'uan,
a distant cliff face towering over scrubby trees
and the tiny cortege, with a waterfall
pouring down the cliff in an unbroken plunge
far above the little wanderers
who head away from it to the scroll's edge;

and in meticulous small painted fans
by Ma Yuan, whose solitary scholars live
in one exquisite moment when the moon
shines through the branches of a fruit tree just in bud,
or sit in contemplation while below
the torrent far beneath them rushes on.

In Japan
(2004)

I
The Temple

Jet-lagged I wander
the almost empty
dawn streets,
enticed to a temple
by the strong vibrations
of a struck gong
and recited sutras.

In a nearby niche
is a life-sized statue
of a bodhisattva
with worn hands,
palms pressed
in the mudra of
salutation.
A frail lady
faces it
and holds her hands
over his.

II
Poetry

In the book enclave
of a gift shop in
the Imperial Hotel,
among the tracts
on efficient management,

I visit the familiar
plop of a frog
in Basho's pond.

III
The Horyu-ji Treasure

A display of mandorlas.
Their engaging flames
invite the eye
to inhabit and hallow
the halo of decoration.

IV
A Priest's Staff

The rings in the finial
tingle so that
every sentience,
each insect,
is warned away
from potential peril.

V
The Fountain

The fountain's white
upright energy
stops, a lapse
lasting to permit
thin ripples
to emanate out of
an unseen center
and slowly spread

to the edges of
the pool's flat
shallow expanse
until there is
stillness.
And then the fountain
commences again.

VI
A Tree

The courtyard encloses
an ancient tree
with a thick trunk
but each leaf
is in its own
convivial quiver.
Who wouldn't want
an endlessly active
rooted unity?

In the British Museum

I
I'm back where we once were, Michèle, where we
once lingered, and I'm looking up at this
ancient granite monument to some
Middle Kingdom pharaoh whose
identity is subject to dispute
under which you stood. I have the photograph.

II
Apparently this crouching simian
carved in quartzite in the Middle Kingdom
was Thoth. Now others are taking photos of
their lovers. Back then it was you, Michèle, near Thoth,
the god of wisdom in the form of a baboon,
a being looking upward with a smile
and a lengthy penis resting on the ground.
I hadn't noticed it those years ago,
and if you did you didn't point it out.
His paws and feet are modeled just like hands,
elegant hands, long fingers like your own
when you and I were alive in this very place
and I took photos of you standing near
the ape, but we were oblivious to all
except ourselves. And that, it turned out, was
our moment with the smiling god of wisdom.

In the Nezu Museum

The subject was one favored by the Academy.
The colors were a black ink's range of tone.
A few wet brush strokes' lush austerity.
Sparrow and Bamboo. The artist is unknown.

No seal of a collector, no colophon.
I stood before it in a suburb of Tokyo
since it stopped me. Then I passed on.
A moment of privilege decades ago.

The Importance of Ecology

"A person of virtue is like bamboo,"
 said Master Li, in a text on painting.
"Its center is a void, like pure humility.
The disposition of its stalks and leaves
is individual, irregular, and yet
all stems stand straight in rectitude
unless bent under pressure, and even then
in release spring back to uprightness."

Did worlds of sturdy solid wooden oaks
that break or are uprooted in a storm
cause worship of strength above resilience?

Once Upon a Time
(*Dhauli*, 260 B.C.E.)

Millennia ago, on the hill of Dhauli,
just as he'd consolidated power
by victory over the kingdom of Kalinga
and ruled all India, Ashoka stood and looked
at the corpses littering the battlefield
and did not fill with pride but, disgusted, saw
dead husbands, brothers, fathers, sons,
and heard the voice of Gautama Sakyamuni,
who'd been a prince too, telling him the Law,
and was converted to the virtue of ahimsa.

Ashoka opened the eight stupas where,
in reliquaries buried at their center,
the ashes of the Buddha were enshrined
with other relics of his mortal life
and had them all divided up again
so eighty thousand stupas could contain
the presence of the Buddha, making it
close to every person in his kingdom,
and placed this Edict where each presence was:

In ages past, during countless centuries,
there was murder, violence to sentient creatures,
but now, by the grace of the practice of the Law
by the king who is a friend of gods of friendship,
what has not yet existed now can be:
kindness to creatures, abstention from their murder.
Practice this Law until the world is ended.
Long live the Law, and those who preach the Law.

His Edict, in a long forgotten script,
was found in the early nineteenth century
by a British gentleman prospecting for coal
who knew and cared enough to inform a scholar.
The scholar was puzzled by the unfamiliar writing
but at last deciphered its tidings of non-violence.

I was the only pilgrim at this isolated site.

Two Calls
(*Genesis 12:1; Exodus 3:55*)

I
To Abraham

Go from your country, kindred, father's house.
Where you are now is not a holy place.
You must obey the imperative to be
dissatisfied. Leave for another you
will only know when you know you have arrived.

II
To Moses

The place on which you stand is holy ground.
Stop. And recognize in a poor thorn bush
like every other you have ever seen
the miracle of the ordinary in flame.

Mencius, More or Less

On a shivering bridge, don't linger for the view;
wait for your fate to take, don't let it take you.

A carpenter can pass on rules of craft.
Can he teach artistry? The Master laughed.

The wild, the squeamish and the middle way:
the wild rush in, the squeamish do not stay.

I teach, but don't go after those who leave;
I weave with whatever thread I have to weave.

Five Careers in the Middle Kingdom
(translated titles are circa 2000 B.C.E.)

I
"I aspire of course to be Overlord of Every Pre-eminent
    Office
but would, if offered, consider Overseer of All Heaven
    Gives
and Earth Creates and the Inundation Brings, but I
will not be fobbed off with Maintainer of the Moon
or some similar trivial juridical position.
Overseer of All Tribute? It's a possibility."

II
"I insinuated into the palace as
Great Chamberlain of the Children, which
(let me whisper this) is just a transition.
When the kids come into their own I won't
be held back by lack of family.
Overseer of the Repast, or perhaps Overseer
of the Offering, is the logical next step,
which, I believe, would even serve
to get me Guardian of the Herds of the Gods,
or Overseer of the Six Courts of Law."

III
"For the time being I am a scribe
but I'm impatient to make the move
to Steward in the future. I'm sick of sitting,
scribbling on shards. I harbor hopes
for Steward of the Storehouse, or Steward of
the Two Jars – I am among the few
who comprehend the import of this position.

I suppose I could live with, though,
Steward Who Reckons Goats."

IV
"I started out as a Fattener of Fowl
but soon flew to become one
of the Embalmers of Anubis, who gives gifts.
Then, with Anubis behind me, I grew
to be a Carrier of the Libation Jar.
Complain? It's been a great career."

V
"I was a Washerman of the Temple and slept
content. At the end I was given permission –
how many, for heaven's sake,
can ever aspire to anything like this? –
to wash the walls, and the floor itself,
of the inner room where the God walks."

Advice
(*from Lui Tao-Ch'un on painting*)

If you're coarse and crude,
strive for refinement;

if delicate and skillful,
struggle for strength;

if untamed, eccentric,
reach for reason;

if dry in manner,
have rich tone.

Predictions That Will Come True
(*The Gospels*)*

In the future:

> *The righteous will be reviled and persecuted.*
>
> *It will rain on the just and the unjust alike.*
>
> *Many will be called but few chosen.*
>
> *Hard men will reap where they have not sowed.*
>
> *To those that have, more will be given.*
>
> *Unprofitable servants will be cast out.*
>
> *The children of this world will be more wise in their generation than the children of light.*
>
> *The Kingdom of Heaven will be within.*

---

* Matt. 5:10-11; Matt. 5:45; Matt. 22:14; Matt. 25:24-6; Matt. 25:29; Matt. 25:30; Luke 16:8; Luke 17:21

Aphorisms in a Sufi Spirit
(*based on the Kitab al-Hikam*)

The Source only pours what the cup can contain.

When a deprivation gives it is a gift.

Not all who pray attain to invocation.

Not all the Elect perfect their fate.

No prayer procures gifts of the spirit.

Gifts from the Non-Contingent are not contingent.

The form of the Formless depends on reception.

Wu Wei
(*for Jeffrey Fiskin*)

At the viewing of an auction of Chinese art
I sat and leafed through an album
quite beyond my capacity to acquire
and stopped. The painting was in a swift
line of dry ink impulsively
switching direction with the brush unlifted
but "heart and hand in accord" to show
a scholar in a garden bowing to
an upright rock much grander than he was
with its own singularity of hollow and prominence
like the painter Wu Wei himself, a Taoist
whose name means *effortless action* and who
was fond of brothels and often intoxicated
and had as a patron even the Emperor.

In the Freer Gallery

A branch of blossoming plum tree, brushed, it appears,
    by flick on flick
of a Yuan wrist, now dead six hundred years
that once was variously skilled and quick.

I walked out with this image in my mind
    my eyes had won,
but they, adjusted to an inner light, were blind
under the dazzle of the lifeless sun.

The Afterlife of Ramesses the Great

The son of Seti, Ramesses the Second, great builder,
defacer of inscriptions of inferior Pharaohs,
husband of a dozen, father of one hundred,
rested as planned for two centuries in the grandeur
of his own tomb, enclosed in a gilded coffin,
until priests, afraid of thieves, shifted him
to a wooden coffin, and small shared quarters.
The mummy was discovered in 1881.

For three thousand years Ramesses hadn't had
his genitals. "They must have dropped off when
the priests re-wrapped him," an expert speculated.
In the Twentieth century, X-rays revealed arthritis,
hardening of the arteries, severe dental problems
and the ravages of bacteria. Sterilized, this time
by radiation – gamma rays – Ramesses is now
freshly prepared for further millennia.

An Ancient Egyptian Lady
(*12th Dynasty, circa 2000* B.C.E.)

She still
stands straight;
her arms are
tight by their sides;
the bones of both
little wrists
are embraced by bracelets;
her fingernails retain
traces of paint;
each ankle
is also adorned;
her lips look
fleshy, full;
her philtrum furrow
is cleanly cut;
her outlined eyes
still glint
of obsidian and,
under her arches,
an extended tenon
still could give
staunch support.
She's as elegant as any
person conceived
in her hereafter.

Classical Moments

Those moments in the Rome
of Horace, Ovid,
Virgil, Propertius,
of Socratic Athens,

of the briefness that created
both the Gupta Buddha
and the Kama Sutra,
were cocooned in the womb

of the brute shrewdness
of Julius Octavian,
now discussed as Augustus,

of the violent raja
renamed Chandragupta,
of the stratigos, General Pericles.

Last Things

Condemned to die
what would I savor
in the cell of the self
as last things?
Imprisoned with me
as icons to ponder
I'd want only objects
created with the aid
of blind nature's
strange ways:
a rock chosen
because eroded
by wind and water
creating furrows
on several faces,
textures devoid
of all design,
a primordial hardness
transformed by
fluid movement;
and the network of crazing
in an ancient pot;
and one with
thick glaze
which was
permitted to trickle.

An Obituary
(*Dr. Judah Folkman*)

At seven he went
with his father, a rabbi,
on pastoral visits
to local hospitals.

He invented an intent –
reduce the blood vessels
that nourish cancer –
and suffered skeptics,

colleagues infatuated
with killing cancer;
he tried to simply

limit it
to be, like life,
a chronic condition.

Yiddish Teleologies

It is said:

In heaven, at the time they were conceived,
the creatures were told exactly how they'd live
and asked to choose the life-span they desired.
The rat, advised he'd scurry round in garbage,
requested brief duration.
The horse, informed he'd be ridden by a master
who'd saddle him and prick his flanks with spurs,
thought twenty years of this more than enough.

I've forgotten what was divulged of how I'd live
(each human is considered a separate creature)
but though free-will prevents perfect prediction
I'm sure that God divined a slog before I'd come
into my own, which could account for my extended life
when so many of my betters have been cut off.

Conjoint Gods
(*Exodus 20:4–5*)

God, in the second commandment, prohibits us
from making graven images of any thing
in the heavens above, or the earth and waters beneath,
or bowing down to those museums display

like the proud alert bronze cats the Egyptians cast
or anthropoid squat good luck gods like Bes
or regal Hatshepsut sitting on her throne
facing eternity with confidence.

But images of imaginary beings
like Sekhmet, with a woman's gorgeous body
and the head of a lioness, are not strictly taboo.

What conjoint god could image me?
Perhaps a mouse with the head of a cat
forever in terror of its appetites.

Babylonian Identities

The Code of Hammurabi required the use
of personal seals for all contracts of trade.
In cylinder seals the figurative prevailed:
man with dagger attacking rampant beast;
worshipper, arms raised, before sacred tree;
priest anointing god standing on dragon;
deity brandishing staff and lightning fork;
winged hero holding feet of upended bull.

If back in fashion what would my seal be?
Cat ignoring man with food in hand?
Suppliant male imploring amused goddess?
Worshipper, arms raised, before the void?
Rational man perusing sacred book?
Hero composing poem in upholstered chair?

The Root of All Evil

By the inventiveness of human intellect
primitive tools replaced much argument:
it was discovered that the hunting club
could manifest the weight of an opinion;
axes could be wielded to chop a block-head off,
and serve as symbols of authority;
the knife was sharpened as a dagger to stab
the index finger jab of emphasis.

The spear, however, was always just a weapon
decked out perhaps by carvings on the shaft
or decorated with elaborate arrays
of fur and feathers positioned up near the blade.
The blade itself became enhanced with barbs
inspired no doubt by verbal barbarity.

Eden, Upstate New York
(*Genesis 2:16–17*)

In a garden filled with shrubs and walnut trees
the owner hung a feeder for small birds.
The local squirrels clambered down the branch
and ate. He fired some BB pellets that said:

Of every tree in my garden thou mayest freely eat
but of this tree with the feeder hanging down
like some exotic fruit, you may not eat
for in the day thou eatest thou shalt surely die.

The squirrels sat and pondered, chattering,
and must have understood since they decided
to stay away, at least while He was there.

Apparently the squirrels said to themselves,
"We're living in Eden here, why risk it all –
the nuts, the berries – for some forbidden food?"

The Life and The Good
(*Deuteronomy 30:15,19*)*

At the end of Deuteronomy we read:
*I set before you this day, the life and the good,
the death and the evil, therefore choose the life.*

I set before you not a mystery
within, but something of concern out there
in the eccentric world confronting you

this day, which is each moment that presents
the life and the good ordained for you
to find, the calling to discern, among

the things that are, those which belong to us,
and not *the death and the evil*, the living death
of refusing to accept the moment's offer.

Choose the life that calls in every moment framed
by what is set before you in the world.

---

* The definite articles are in the Hebrew but not in standard translations.

Before the Throne of Judgment

On my mother's side, the exit mode preferred
at the unforeseeable and fated time
which I have faith will be a few years off
is the heart attack, after which, so I assume,
I'll find myself before the Throne of Judgment.
Rabbi Meshullam Zusya of Hanipol,
disciple of an even greater man,
the wandering preacher known as the Great Maggid,

a disciple of the Baal Shem Tov himself,
as he was dying, said, "I will be asked
one question only, not 'Why didn't you
mature into another Moses?' but
'Why didn't you become Meshullam Zusya?'"
Who wouldn't beg for mercy from that court?

The Theology of the Big Bang
(*Primo Levi*)

Though ancient sages speculated on
what could have caused the world's fecundity
we now believe all manifested things,
stars and galaxies, black holes, the earth,

the continents that formed as it cooled down,
whatever was the first embodiment,
the compound eyes of trilobites,
the uniqueness of each species killed off in

the mass extinctions, Adam and Eve in Africa,
the first migrations to the Middle East
of creatures who could conceive of the divine,

the opening of Genesis, and you
and me, and what comes after us,
were there in potential in the great explosion.

If You Do Well
(*Genesis 4:4–7*)

And the Lord had respect for Abel's offering
but for Cain and his offering He had no respect.
And Cain was very angry and his face fell.
And the Lord said, "If you do well it will be lifted up."

To what may this be compared? Three parables:

I
When Cain and Abel were twenty they enrolled
in a life class at the Academy of Art.
The instructor walked around the class and stopped
to look at Abel's drawing and remarked, "You have
God-given talent, Abel." But when he looked
at Cain's he didn't speak and started to move on.
And Cain's face fell. And the instructor said, "If you
keep on you'll learn, and from this perseverance,
to use a Biblical phrase, you will be lifted up;
perhaps with effort you'll come into your own."

II
When Cain and Abel were thirty they brought their
    slides
to the owner of a well-known gallery.
The owner looked at Abel's offering
and said, "I have been following your career;
I'd like to represent you. Let's have lunch."
But after looking over what Cain brought
he said, "These aren't for us." And Cain's face fell.
And the owner said, "Surely you know by now
there's no equality of talent, Cain.
You're not Picasso. You want to be an artist

so dedicate yourself and it will lift you up."

III
Cain and Abel are forty, and both are artists.
Abel is well-known, and Cain is not.
The brothers go together for a check-up.
Their doctor says to Abel, "God has given you
the constitution of an ox and even though
you drink too much and never exercise
you're fine. You'll probably be giving us
your paintings for another forty years."
Then the doctor turned to Cain and said, "This is
always hard. Your cancer has come back
and you have only months, not years, to live."
And Cain's face fell. And the doctor said, "If you
give in to bitterness you will corrode
the last stage of your life. But if you face
your death with dignity, then, in the phrase
given to your namesake, it will be lifted up."

Make an Ark
(*Genesis 6:5–13; 8:21*)

Before the flood, God noticed, with a sigh,
the wickedness of man was great in the earth
and every imagination of the thoughts of his heart
was only evil, for the earth is filled

with violence, and decided He would make
a future New World Order with the few
who would survive His deluge of the past.
But after the world was reduced to mud and corpses

the Lord Himself acknowledged He had failed,
for the imagination of man's heart is evil from his youth.
The corrupt old order re-assumed its sway.

Make an ark, it seems, is the best God could suggest.
All we can hope to have, like Noah, is
a short-lived sense of floating above it all.

The Existential Ant
(*Deuteronomy 30:11–12*)

*For this commandment which I command you this day
is not too hard for you. It is not in heaven.*
To what may this be compared? To a path on which

we pour a glob of honey ahead of some ants.
We straighten up again, loom over them.
In the midst of its companions each ant is alone.

This one will get stuck in honey, that one won't.
The problem is down there, before each ant,
not here in heaven, six feet up in the sky,

The Need to Dissemble

Freud tells us we don't mind "the smell of our
excreta" but only that of other people since
some animal past is preserved in mental life;
that any heart laid bare is not a charming sight;
that we need rigid customs to constrain
the onslaught of incarnate impulses.
And Baudelaire, in his unpublished notes
for a preface to *Les Fleurs du Mal*, admits
that artists don't explain to what extent
sincerity is mixed with artifice in art;
that originality is based on imitation;
that surprise requires prior monotony;
that inspiration is a vanity and danger;
that his only purpose was to amuse himself.

Blessings and Curses
(*Deuteronomy 11:26*)

I set before you this day a blessing and a curse.
That is our universal circumstance.

Did Madame Bovary or Anna Karenina
suffer from poverty or physical abuse?
Those heroines felt trapped by marriage to
devotion, comfort and security
but in the new lives they elicited
the blessings and the curses were extreme.

The dilemmas of staying on or choosing change
are much the same for all the fortunate.
To stay is to retain known blessings and known curses,
to change is to acquire another set.
There's mutilation at the heart of every moment;
each choice kills off a multitude of selves.

The Days of the Years of Your Life
(*Genesis 47:8*)

How many are the days of the years of thy life?
Was Pharaoh asking Jacob how many days
remained in vivid memory out of all his years?
Had Jacob answered he could have recalled
the wedding night when Leah was in his bed;
the day he saw the blood-stained coat of Joseph;
the night he was alone and wrestled with a man
on the bank of the Jabbok River at its ford.

And in *The Prelude*, Wordsworth gives moment to
the "spots of time" when nature spoke to him;
and Wyatt recalls a loose gown falling from
lovely shoulders; and for Kamienska there was
a path with patches of sunlight on which she ran
when she was six, that stayed until the end.

Loving Your Neighbor
(*Leviticus 19:18; Analects 5:11*)

In Kovno, in September nineteen forty-one,
the Council of Jewish Elders was ordered to
distribute several hundred permit cards.
Each card to a neighbor meant some other
would die. The Council asked Rav Oshry if
they should obey. The Talmud had both views
but Oshry ruled if they could save a life
they had to summon up the spirit to do so.

Love your neighbor as yourself: I am the Lord.
Even in easy times it isn't simple.
Tzu-kung said to the Master, "What I do not want
others to do to me, I've no desire
to do to them." Confucius laughed and said,
"Oh, Ssu! You haven't got to that stage yet."

Benedictions

On twenty-nine October nineteen forty-one,
in Kovno, thirty thousand ghetto Jews
were rounded up for a *selektion* by the Germans.
Reb Elyah, who had fled from Poland, was
in the crowd of those unfortunates
and came to Rabbi Oshry to inquire
the proper form of benediction to be
recited as the murdering began.

He wanted to pass among the throng
in the *Demokratia Platz* and teach it to the others.
Surely those who found themselves concerned
with the form of blessing to say while being murdered
were living hallowed lives. And as for us,
the abundance of the world will have to do.

Justice
(*Deuteronomy 16:20*)

Justice, justice shall you pursue, that you may thrive.
How can this repetition be justified?
Can justice be so problematical?

Psalm thirty-three says God "loves righteousness
and justice" so this distinction should apply.
The repetition tells us justice is

to be preferred if there is any doubt.
Isaiah instructs us to "seek justice and relief
of the oppressed." Could these two be opposed?

The gulags were in the name of the oppressed.
Stalin and Mao were sure of their righteousness.
They, in the phrase of Amos, "turned justice into gall."

Ten Other Commandments

The Torah has all these,* as well as those:

Be fruitful and multiply and replenish the earth.

You shall not follow a multitude to do evil.

You shall not favor a poor man in his cause.

You shall not curse the deaf nor put a stumbling-block before the blind.

You shall not favor the person of the mighty.

You shall love your neighbor as yourself.

You do not live by bread alone.

You shall not harden your heart nor shut your hand.

You shall rejoice in all the good that's given to you.

Let it suffice.

---

* Genesis 9:1; Exodus 23:2, 23.3; Leviticus 19:14, 19:15, 19:18; Deuteronomy 8:3, 15:7, 26:11, 3:26.

Four of Freud's Antiquities

A late dynastic bronze of the god Ptah
who created the world by speech and thought alone.

A Babylonian bearded god of omens who
cuts through the dark with a distinctive blade.

A faience beetle that lays its eggs in dung
from which eventually life can emerge.

A Roman Period marble ape named Thoth
who holds the scales on which the heart is weighed.

Gods of the "A" List
(*reading an encyclopedia*)

Injustice had a goddess, who was Greek.
The ugly *Adikia* is usually depicted
with *Dike*, the goddess of justice, attempting,
apparently without success, to strangle her.
Dike herself was an attractive woman
abused by men but honored by the gods.

The Roman god *Aequitas*, the spirit of
fair play, was regarded as a minor deity,
never as powerful as the major gods.

Apollo, patron of poets, was god of both
healing and pestilence, a natural combination.

Abandinus was a Celtic god who had,
and I admire him for it, unknown affinities.

The Greeks and Romans were careful to also worship,
in plural form, as prudence would dictate,
Agnostos Theos, the unknown among the gods.

A Cold Palm Reading

I have you in my mind, unknown reader,
and now will venture a tentative cold reading.

I'll start with facts you comprehend are true
but do not quite acknowledge in yourself:

You are considerate, but there have been times
of surprise at how self-centered you've become.

You are unnecessarily defensive;
lower defenses would rarely have caused harm.

You've been meticulous with trivia
and yet were careless with an important task.

Thoughts of plans formed in youthful confidence
disturb you more than you have cared to think.

Both of us know all your capacities
have not been adequately used. Some still could be.

You give to reason more scope than you should;
your intuition often has proved right.

Most people, even those you love, don't always
understand what means the most to you.

I sense you nearing a profound transition
but it is dark, I can't discern the other side.

The Insects

I envy the insects   for several reasons:
metamorphosis gives them   surprising lives,
quite different existences   in fixed stages,
obviating the danger   of neurotic stops;
the insect integument   is flexible but strong
unlike our skin   so simple to prick;
even adults aren't   morally responsible,
a bee's sting isn't   an aggressive act,
stimulus and instinct   is not free will
so God wasn't teasing   as He was with us.
No wonder the most abundant   phylum by far,
are the arthropods,   and the class *Insecta*
has more than half   of all animals.
Their mouth-parts can pierce,   rasp, sponge,
lap, lacerate,   siphon, suck.
So many modes   of receptive delectation!

The Auction of Lot 68

"Let me be clear: this one, while not antique,
is old enough to be considered vintage.

It has its nicks and scratches, cracks and chips,
and dark discoloration in several places;

light wear and other minor losses at the edges;
small signs of shrinkage in both sides and back,

and the expected fills and restorations;
and the joinery is loose and needs some care;

and some soft sections are replacements of
the strong originals, but, overall,

considering its age, the condition is
remarkable, and it has a fine patina.

Does no one want to live with such a vintage?
Last call. All done? Are there no regrets?
           Passed."

Is It Worship?

When a troop of chimps
moving through
a gloomy forest
discern a distant
dense steady
unseen sound
and are drawn toward it

and emerge to confront
all at once
a weight of water
in roaring
        fall
and see this force
is haloed by
rainbows of spray

their body hair
bristles before
a presence which
incites a stamping
dance to what
I divine they believe
animates its nature.

Cardiovascular Facts and Fates

The total count of heart beats in the life
of mouse and elephant is much the same,
about a billion and a half when all
is squeaked, or trumpeted, and done.

The squeaker's heart beats seven hundred times,
the trumpeter's a measly twenty-eight,
for every minute of their mortal lives.
One scampers, the other lumbers ponderously on.

A small short life of quick heart beats
that flees when frightened into its retreats
would not appeal to a greatness that rarely knows defeats

and the lumbering trumpeter has a more complex brain
but would a scamp trade life in the fast lane
for a heart so indolent, a voice so vain?

Why Bring Us Here to Die?
(*Exodus 14:10–15*)

God said to Moses at the Sea:
"Go forward; why do they cry out to Me?

Let them remove resistance from their heart;
isn't that how every act must start?

They've got to have belief in order to advance;
their genes are merely the effects of chance.

They ask, 'Why bring us here to die?'
Why keep on asking why?"

Scholar Rocks

For meditative Chinese petrophiles
rocks are a genre composed
by potent and cogent powers
that fabricate lucid forms

from fluent flows of magma
cooling to compressed patterns
or sedimentary deposition
shaped by shearing, erosion.

Images of these energies are known
to those who contemplate a rock's
textures, depths, projections.

As an ancient manual asks,
*Can a cultivated painter portray
a rock that lacks spirit?*

Someone Explains Himself

Once upon a time on a frigid winter day
some hedgehogs tried to keep the cold at bay
but cozying up for warmth meant the pricks were mean
and at safe distance the freezing air flowed in between.

An isolated hedgehog tucked in its toes
and lived by the fire in its belly. I am one of those.

It's Been One Year
(*i.m.* Diane Bailey, 1950–2015)

I
I went to China six weeks before you died.
Your voice was clear and adamant on the phone:
"Don't worry, and don't cut the visit short.
We'll meet at the treatment after you return."

You liked a restaurant on the Cancer Center's block.
I got there early, watched the door. It was a shock.
You hobbled, leaning on a walking-stick.
The cancer had crippled you while I was gone.
Your stable nature now contained this fitfulness.
I was glad to hear you still had appetite.
And then we hesitantly walked along the street.
The radiation didn't take much time.
In the elevator you held onto my arm.
You argued you could get home by yourself.
You'd catch the bus. We took the cab I hailed.
The driver waited patiently as you painfully eased in.
The seat was soft and you managed to sink back.
You were heading for your haven and relaxed.
The traffic slowed to a stop, but started up again.
It was a comforting enclosure for us both.

And then your end. A bed in a hospital.
You couldn't move or speak. Your limbic hours.
I looked into your eyes. My last words were absurd:
"I wish that there was something I could say."
The pupils of your eyes grew wider in response.
You were amused I couldn't find a thought.
This riposte was your parting gift to me:
it gave a radiance as my last sense of you.

And then the coma. Your body was wheeled out
and driven in an ambulance back home
to those extended days of breathing heavily
as your vital constitution contended on
while watched and washed by family and friends.

II
And yesterday, the first anniversary of
your death, I went to walk in Central Park
with all the audience, and the actors too,
from scene to scene, in one of Shakespeare's plays,
as you and I had done in summers of our past.
And this year, acting in a Midsummer Dream,
an Oberon conjured his sleeping Queen:
> *Be as thou wast wont to be;*
> *See as thou wast wont to see.*
> *Dian's bud o'er Cupid's flower*
> *Hath such force and blessèd power.*

Three Consolations
(*Dong Qichang, 1555–1636*)

The artist who no longer needs to charm
can then disarm.

After the erudite dexterities
can come an ease.

We must traverse the mountain to attain
a further plain.

The Life You Had
(*Deuteronomy 3:23–26*)

The pleas of Moses just before he died
provoked the Lord to remind him of the facts:
"Some people, as Cavafy will observe,
have the great Yes within them ready to say

but at the Burning Bush you wanted to
say the great No, like every honest prophet.
I had to drag Yes out of you against your will,
that Yes which led to your accomplishments.

Don't think they were your own. Please keep in mind
the little miracles throughout your life.
Without that Yes, and them, you would have been
a shepherd in Midian who said his No.

And now you want to see, and cross into,
the promised land! Let the life you had suffice."

Acknowledgments

Some of the poems in this collection have appeared in the following books:

Midrashim by David Curzon, published as Chapbook No. 5 in the Jewish Writers Series: Cross Cultural Communications, 1991
Chapters into Verse: Poetry in English Inspired by the Bible edited by Robert Atwan and Laurence Wieder: Oxford University Press, 1993
Modern Poems on the Bible: An Anthology edited by David Curzon: The Jewish Publication Society of America, 1994
The Oxford Book of Australian Religious Verse edited by Kevin Hart: Oxford University Press, 1994
The Gospels in Our Image: An Anthology of Twentieth-Century Poetry Based on Biblical Texts edited by David Curzon: Harcourt, Brace and Company, 1995
The View from Jacob's Ladder: One Hundred Midrashim by David Curzon: The Jewish Publication Society of America, 1996
Dovchik by David Curzon: Penguin Books Australia, 1996
Beyond Lament: Poets of the World Bearing Witness to the Holocaust edited by Marguerite M. Striar: Northwestern University Press, 1998
World Poetry: An Anthology of Verse from Antiquity to

Our Time edited by Katharine Washburn and John S. Major: Norton, 1998

And in the following journals:

USA: *Agenda, Antaeus, Antipodes, Central Park, Forward, HaDoar* (in Hebrew trans.), *Long Island Quarterly, New Menorah, New Republic, Pivot, Poetry, Sewanee Review, Shenandoah, Tikkun, Western Humanities Review, Wigwag;* AUSTRALIA: *Overland, Westerly;* ISRAEL: *The Jerusalem Review, Tel Aviv Review;* UK: *The Jewish Quarterly*

About the Author

David Curzon was born in Melbourne. He has a B.Sc. in physics and obtained a doctorate in economics for a dissertation entitled "An Axiomatic Approach to the Study of Responsibility in Choice" which is heavy enough to stabilize the shaky bookshelf where he keeps poetry. He has traveled around the world many times, followed Vinoba Bhave in India, seen Angkor Wat and Pompeii and the pyramids of the Sun and the Moon, had a wedding in Jerusalem and a divorce in New York, worked for the Commonwealth Scientific and Industrial Research Organization in Australia and the National Aeronautics and Space Administration in Washington, and as a professor of economics, and in the United Nations where, as Chief of the Central Evaluation Unit, he assessed the effectiveness of its activities, including peacekeeping operations and the refugee and environment programs. He takes comfort in Rilke's remark that "for the sake of a single verse one must see many cities, people, and things."

Mr. Curzon has published two previous books of poetry, *Midrashim* and *Dovchik*; a collection of poetry and prose, *The View from Jacob's Ladder*; and two anthologies of twentieth-century poetry based on biblical texts, *Modern Poems on the Bible* and *The Gospels in Our Image*.

www.ingramcontent.com/pod-product-compliance
Lightning Source LLC
LaVergne TN
LVHW041340080426
835512LV00006B/545